**This book is dedicated to my mum
and husband Richard.**

*We miss my mum every day; she told me I should write
a book and I hope she would have been proud.*

*Richard my very patient husband, who is as excited about this
book as I am and walks with me all over the moors.*

To Wayne & Denise,
Enjoy Dartmoor.
Best wishes
Denise
(and Winnie)

Walks with Winnie

By Denise Horner
Illustrated and designed by Sara Nunan

Scorhill Stone Circle at sunset

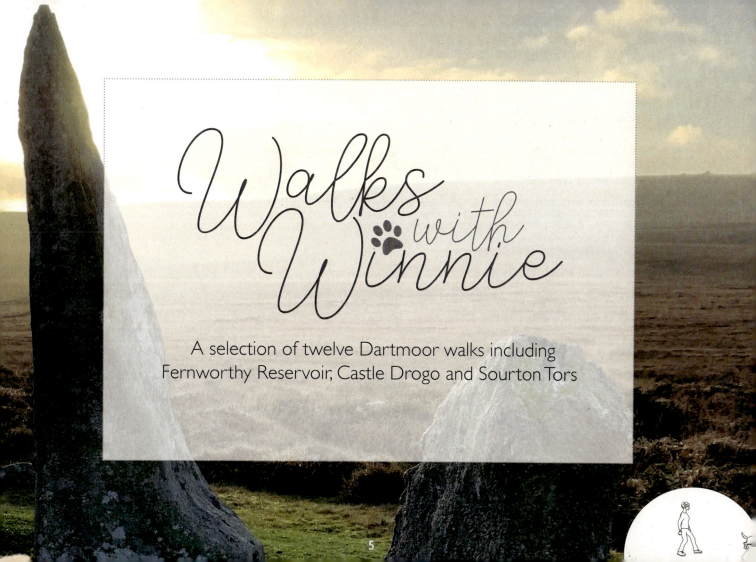

Walks with Winnie

A selection of twelve Dartmoor walks including Fernworthy Reservoir, Castle Drogo and Sourton Tors

Author Denise Horner
Illustrator and Art Editor Sara Nunan
Animated flick book Claudia Aaron
Photography Sara Nunan, Denise and Richard Horner
Proof readers Frances Goudge and David Lewin
Printed by Hedgerow Print, Crediton, Devon, UK
Printed on 100% recycled Nautilus offwhite 300/120gsm paper
Designed and packaged by LittleLinenBook
First published in Great Britain, December 2020
Copyright walks with winnie©

ISBN 978-1-80049-013-0

⬚ walkswithwinnie on Dartmoor
www.walkswithwinnie.co.uk

⬚ walkswithwinnie on Dartmoor
winnie@walkswithwinnie.co.uk

⬚ dartmoorbnordicwalking
www.dartmoornordicwalking.co.uk

⬚ dartmoornordicwalking
denise@dartmoornordicwalking.co.uk

KEY

what3words /// The website, what3words.com. Every 3m² of the world has been given a unique combination of 3 words. We use these 3 words for the starting point of each walk.

·················· Walking route.

△ Triangulation (Trig) point.

▲ Height marker in metres.

 easy   medium   difficult

(All walks are suitable for an average level of fitness with some walks being more challenging than others.)

Rowtor looking towards West Mill Tor

Contents

Fernworthy Reservoir 13

Castle Drogo 17

Batworthy Corner 23

Scorhill 27

Belstone Cleave 31

Meldon Reservoir 35

Whiddon Deer Park 41

Cosdon Beacon 45

Halstock Bluebell Woods 49

Fatherford 53

High Willhays 57

Corn Ridge WWII Crash site 61

Glossary 64

Winnie and Denise with High Willhays in the background

Introduction

Having written the "Walks with Winnie" for the Oke Links Magazine, I realised that many people followed our adventures. As the groups I take out on the moors walking liked to find new routes, I decided that putting a selection of walks into a book was the next obvious step. There are 12 stunning walks, taking in locations from Fernworthy Reservoir, Castle Drogo and Sourton Tors. The walks, varying in difficulty, terrain and views, are great walks for you and your dog to enjoy. If you have the time, you could actually link all 12 walks together!

The walks are very descriptive; there are interesting facts with the walks, beautifully illustrated maps (not to scale or to be used for navigation purposes; for guidance only) and photos taken along the route. I don't pretend to be an expert on Dartmoor History or expect the reader to be able to use a map and compass, however, when walking on Dartmoor, you always need to be prepared with the correct kit, clothing, footwear and have checked the weather. Take a detailed map with you and let someone know where you are going.

Dartmoor and its weather can be unpredictable, even in the summer.

We hope you enjoy reading this book and walking the walks as much as we do.

Denise and Winnie

Belstone Tor *(opposite)*

Belstone Tor and Irishman's Wall

- Fernworthy Reservoir
- Castle Drogo

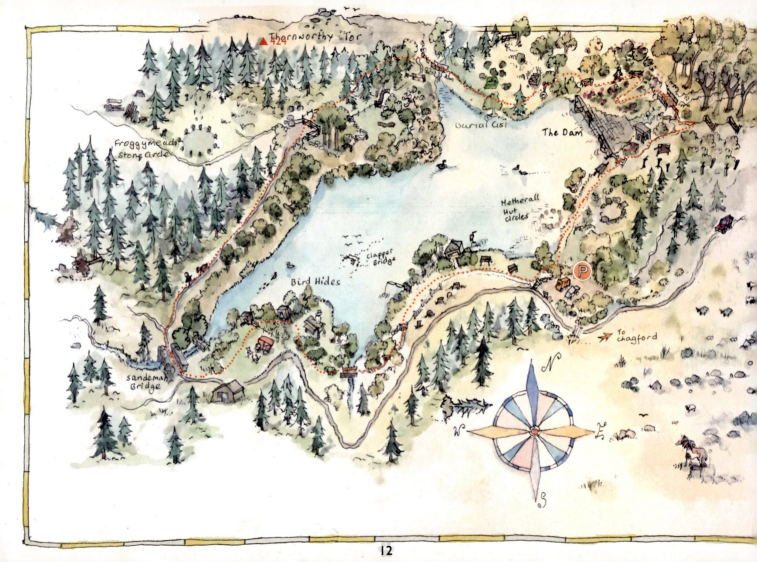

Fernworthy Reservoir

> **DISTANCE** *Approximately 4.5km (2.8miles)* **TIME** *Allow 1hr.*
> **DIFFICULTY** *Mostly level surface with easy going terrain. Can be muddy in places after rain. Fernworthy Reservoir Car Park, is now pay and display.*
> /// **WHAT3WORDS** *ratio.sparkle.irrigate or SX669838*
> **WINNIE SAYS** *this is a* 🐾

A circular walk around Fernworthy Reservoir, starting and finishing at the Car Park. When you arrive you will be treated to an amazing view across the reservoir towards Thornworthy Tor, a walk for another day! Although the reservoir looks most inviting for a swim, unfortunately neither dogs or humans are allowed.

Fernworthy Reservoir is in **Dartmoor National Park** managed by South West Lakes and was completed in 1942. There are toilet facilities at the car park, closed during the winter months, open from April onwards.

The Potter's Walk is an alternative shorter 1.1km, Wheel Chair accessible walk that also starts and finishes at the car park. There is a map on the side of the toilet block showing the route.

With the reservoir in front of you, take the track to the bottom right of the car park and head over the small bridge.

A burial cist

Walks with Winnie

After about 50m on your right hand side you will easily see **Metherall Hut Circles**, especially during the winter when the bracken has died back and if the water levels are low, you will also be able to see further hut circles at the edge of the water on your left hand side.

Continue on the path, through the gate by the dam, looking for the path between the bushes on your left hand side, taking you down to the river and the base of the reservoir. A great spot to see the flow of the water over the edge of the dam and a chance for the dog to have a swim. This is the South Teign River.

Follow the path to the right winding up the slope towards the top of the dam. The path will then take you around the wall and along the edge of the reservoir, this section can sometimes become quite muddy. However, it has recently been laid with gravel.

Stay on this path until you come to a narrow bridge, cross this and take the small gate to your left continuing to the next gate with **Fernworthy Forest** on your right hand side.

The path is clearly marked through a section of forest along a boardwalk, coming to a lovely opening in to a field with views across the reservoir. A great place to be at one with nature, keep your eyes open for butterflies. Walk straight across this first and then a second field. If the water levels are low, look left towards the water and you may get to see a small clapper bridge that is normally submerged. Last seen clearly in 2016.

Metherall hut circles. Normally under water unless the water levels are low

Pearl bordered fritillary

Fernworthy Reservoir

The bridge that is normally submerged and last seen in 2016

Arriving at the five bar gate on your right, proceed through this and the next one in front of you on to the road; the furthest point that you can drive to around Fernworthy. On the right here you will see access to the forest and more walks to explore, where you will find **Fernworthy Circle** at Froggymead, Stone Rows, hut circles and more.

Stay on the road until you come to a large building on your right hand side. Opposite it you will see a gateway into the field. There is a bird hide inside the gate on your left; worth a visit. Walking down towards the water is a great spot for a picnic where you will find a bench and better views of the bridge. If the water is low you can walk over it. The path will then continue around the edge of the water, over a small bridge into the forest walking along a clear path on the boardwalk. The path then takes you further into the forest bringing you out into an area recently cleared of trees, giving views of the reservoir on your left and Thornworthy Tor. A gateway will then take you back on a gravel track to the car park. The picnic benches will be waiting for you to rest, enjoy the view and have a cup of tea from your flask!

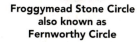

Froggymead Stone Circle also known as Fernworthy Circle

Did you know....

Outdoor exercise provides a mental health boost beyond that of indoor gyms. Moving outdoors has been shown to reduce anger and depression and improve mood (Barton and Pretty, 2010).

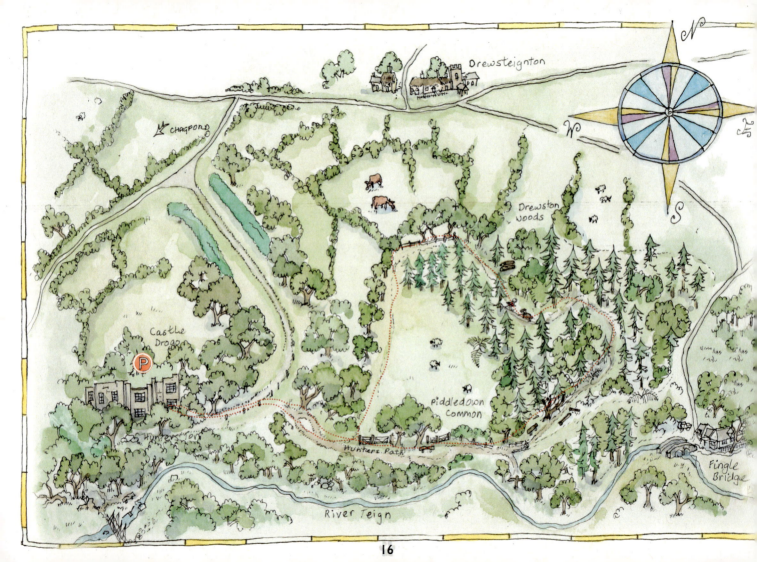

Castle Drogo

DISTANCE *Approximately 5km (3miles).* **TIME** *Allow 1.5hrs.*
DIFFICULTY *Flat in parts but there are hills. Nordic Walking poles will help.*
///**WHAT3WORDS** *operating.depend.storming or SX724903*
WINNIE SAYS *this is a* 🐾

This is a circular walk starting and finishing at **Castle Drogo** car park. Parking is free if you are a member of the **National Trust**. There are cafe, shop and toilet facilities by the car park, with doggie poo bins towards the start of the walk. There are seats all the way along this route to relax and enjoy the view. The views are breathtaking!

With the car park behind you, head out of the entrance of the car park and turn immediately left, crossing the road and

One of the many seats along the walk to enjoy the view from

walking along the path on the right hand side. By the sign and noticeboard, take the path toward the open grass space on the left through the small set of trees; not down to your right. In the open space take the higher path in front of you as you look towards the moors on your right, with a view of Castle Drogo in front, and **Hunter's Tor** just below it. You can also see **Whiddon Deer Park** on the left across the valley…a walk for another day. Stay on this path, through a gate until it

Walks with Winnie

Entrance to Castle Drogo

This path will take you through Drewston Common and Woods, passing a very large Oak tree on your left. The path continues to the right through a gate following a woodland path until you reach a crossroads of tracks with a "Path" sign on the right. Head straight over staying on this track and enjoy the views and colours of the woodland. The 'Hunters path' sign will appear on your right, turn immediately left and then first right on the grassy track climbing up hill. Poles would be good at this point! This track takes you along the top of the

Large old oak tree

takes you down a small slope to join a path from the right. Turn left and follow this higher path with views across the valley again, with the River Teign below and **Cranbrook Castle Hill Fort** in the distance. Carry on through a gate until you come to a fork in the path. Take the top path left; now the **Hunters Path**. (Taking the right path will take you down to Fingle Bridge).

The signpost at the fork in the path also part of Dartmoor Way

Castle Drogo

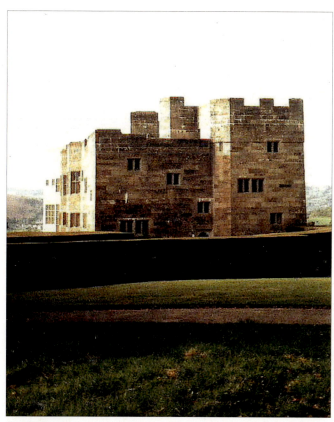

Castle Drogo

woods with views to your right of Drewsteighton and the Church. At each of the next two "Piddledown" signs, take a left again up hill until you reach a gate at the edge of the woods.

Through the gate you will now enter a field which may have cattle or sheep in. Head straight up the hill, keeping the fence on your right hand side. At the brow of this hill you will have an even better view of Drewsteighton behind you. Continue through another field gate and down towards a wooden gate. This will now bring you back to the path you started on. Turn right here and head back towards the Castle, cafe and well deserved tea and cake, enjoying the views as you go.

You may find that taking this walk in the opposite direction feels less hilly as the climbs are more gradual!

Did you know...

Nordic walking technique with Nordic Walking poles can enhance the energy you are using when walking by 45%. This is because you are using over 90% of your muscles therefore burning more energy and as a result using more calories.

Scorhill Stone Circle

- Batworthy Corner
- Scorhill
- Belstone Cleave
- Meldon Reservoir

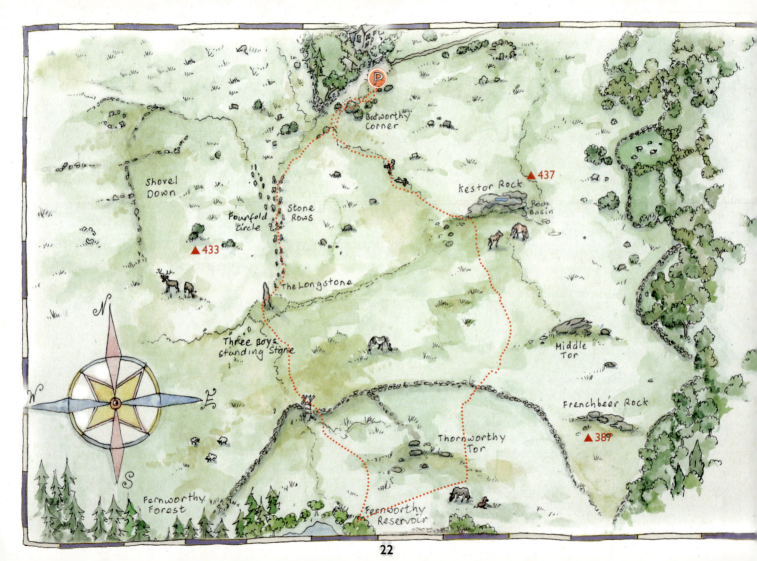

Batworthy Corner

> **DISTANCE** *Approximately 6km (3.7miles).* **TIME** *Approximately 1.5-2hrs.*
> **DIFFICULTY** *A medium level of difficulty, with a few gentle hills. The ground can be uneven and boggy in places.*
> ///**WHAT3WORDS** *improvise.drop.eager or SX663865*
> **WINNIE SAYS** *this is a* 🐾🐾

This is an open moor walk starting at Batworthy Corner near Kestor. The walk takes you from Kestor to Thornworthy Tor, Thornworthy Down, the edge of Fernworthy Reservoir and return via **Three Boys Standing Stone** and stone rows on the edge of Shovel Down. The views are impressive all the way round. A really great dog walk.

You can drive all the way to a small bridge with a parking area on the left before Batworthy. There is no right of way through Batworthy. Park here although please note: it is a small car park.

With the bridge to your right, head up on to the moors keeping the stone wall on your right hand side. There is a track here to follow until you reach the corner of the stone wall, (Batworthy Corner) where you will see Kestor up and on your left. Follow the clear path up to the Tor. The views from the top are astounding across to Chagford, Middle Tor, Shovel Down and beyond.

Kestor from Batworthy Corner

Walks with Winnie

Kestor and the rock basin *(right)*

be very boggy; more so in the winter or after heavy rain so tread carefully. Head up to the top of the tor picking your way over the rocks. The views once you arrive are amazing and far reaching to **Fernworthy Reservoir** and beyond.

As you look at Fernworthy Reservoir, you will see a stone wall on your left heading down towards it. This is now Thornworthy Down. Head for the corner of the wall and the gates. If you would like to make the walk longer, you can head through the gates towards the reservoir and follow the path either right or left here and walk all the way around. This would then be the Fernworthy Reservoir walk on page 13.

At the top of the Tor is a natural **rock basin** usually full of water. It is said that it was used by the Druids to catch blood from human sacrifices!

Standing with Kestor to your right and Middle Tor to your left you will see Thornworthy Tor in front of you looking more like a hill than a Tor. There are a couple of paths ahead of you, take the one slightly right heading towards the tor where you will see a stile in the wall. The ground either side of the wall can

Now you are heading back from the gates, head towards Thornworthy Tor but instead of walking up to the tor, take a path that contours around the bottom edge heading left which will

Purple heather grows abundantly on the moor

Batworthy Corner

Stone Rows at Shoveldown

The Langstone also known as the Long Stone

bring you to a stream, where you will see lots of scars on the land. Looking ahead and towards the wall is another gate, head through this up the hill but take the path veering right, leading towards Three Boys Standing Stone and **'Langstone'** or **Long Stone** which will be seen on its own in the middle of 2 stone rows at Shovel Down. There is so much to see here including 5 double stone rows, a single stone row and the Fourfold Circle, a configuration of 4 concentric stone circles.

With the 'Langstone' on your left, take the path straight in front of you passing the stone rows, following the direction of the stone row slightly right, head back towards Batworthy Corner. You can see Kestor on the horizon to your right. Keep the wall on your left and head back towards the car. The views always look different in the opposite direction.

Did you know....

Dartmoor has the largest concentrations of stone rows of any area in Britain. There are over seventy stone rows known on Dartmoor today although there were probably once considerably more.

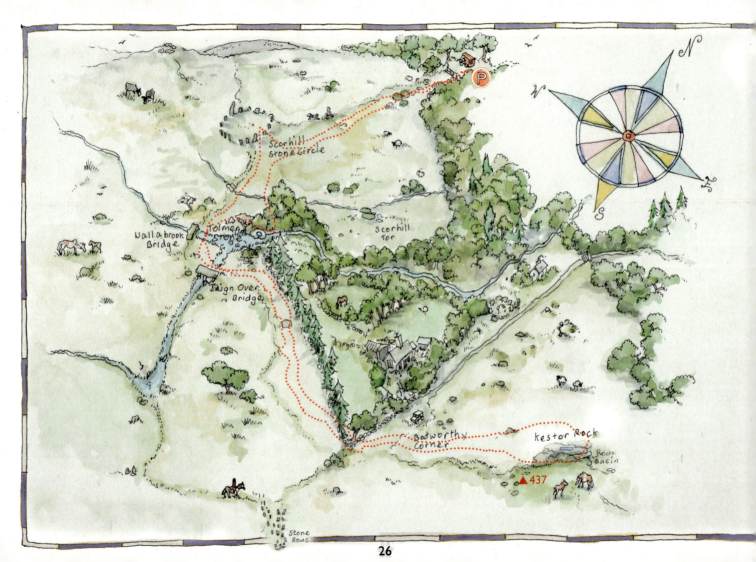

Scorhill

> **DISTANCE** *Approximately 6km (3.7miles)* **TIME** *Approximately 1hr40mins.*
> *It may take longer as there is a lot to see*
> **DIFFICULTY** *Hilly, but smooth ones!*
> ///**WHAT3WORDS** *starting.florists.universal* or *SX664879*
> **WINNIE SAYS** *this is a* 🐾 🐾

Teign-e-ver Clapper Bridge

The car park at Scorhill is rather small so it can be hard to find a space at busy times of the year. Be aware that this is private land so please park appropriately.

Scorhill to Kestor and return, taking in the **Tolmen Stone** (reputed to have healing powers) and **Scorhill Stone Circle**. This is an open walk, so do be aware of the weather. Plenty of places for the dogs and you to swim though!

From the car park, take the gate on to the moors and follow the track left and up the hill. The path will bring you out onto the open moor where you will have panoramic views from left to right of Scorhill Tor, Kestor, Ferworthy Forest, Watern Tor, Wild Tor, Steeperton Tor in the far distance and Cosdon Beacon to your far right.

The track will then take you down the hill towards North Teign River, but before that you will see Scorhill Stone

Walks with Winnie

Scorhill Stone Circle

Circle situated to your right at Gidleigh Common. Also know as Gidleigh Stone Circle or Steep Hill Stone Circle. It supposedly had 70-80 original standing stones but now has only 34 left. It is said you cannot lead livestock or horses through it. It is Bronze Age, has not been restored and is one of seven in this area lying roughly 2km apart.

Walk back from the circle, head towards the river taking in the **leat** on your right, and cross the stone bridge. Continue on the path down towards the Wallabrook and the Wallabrook **Clapper Bridge**, approaching the North Teign River via the Teign-e-ver Clapper Bridge. Two clapper bridges in one spot!

Take the path slightly left which runs parallel to the stone wall by the woods, continuing to the corner of the wall; this is Batworthy Corner from where you will see Kestor. Stay on the nice wide path all the way up to the tor. The views from here are far reaching and extraordinary. You can easily see Fernworthy Forest where the reservoir is and feel you could keep going for miles.

View from Kestor

28

Scorhill

Heading back the way you came to Batworthy Corner, head for Teign-e-ver Clapper Bridge again, then after crossing the Wallabrook Clapper Bridge, turn immediately right, keeping close to the water's edge until you are standing opposite the end of the stone wall on the other side of the river. You will then have come to the **Tolmen Stone**; A large stone with a hole in that you can actually climb through. You may need to be a bit agile though! The stone is said to have healing powers to cure various aliments.

Leaving the stone behind you, track back to the left the way you have come, keeping the river on your left.

Tolmen Stone; said to have healing powers or even make you pregnant if you climb through it

Head up hill over the leat taking the wide path back towards the car. Take time to stop at the brow of the hill and admire the 360 degree views. This is one of the most visited areas on Dartmoor, by people from all over the world.

You will eventually meet the path which will take you back to your car.

Did you know....

Today it is estimated that there are around 200 clapper bridges still spanning Dartmoor's waters and for a fact many more have disappeared. You will see 2 of them on this walk.

The granite bridge with metal straps

29

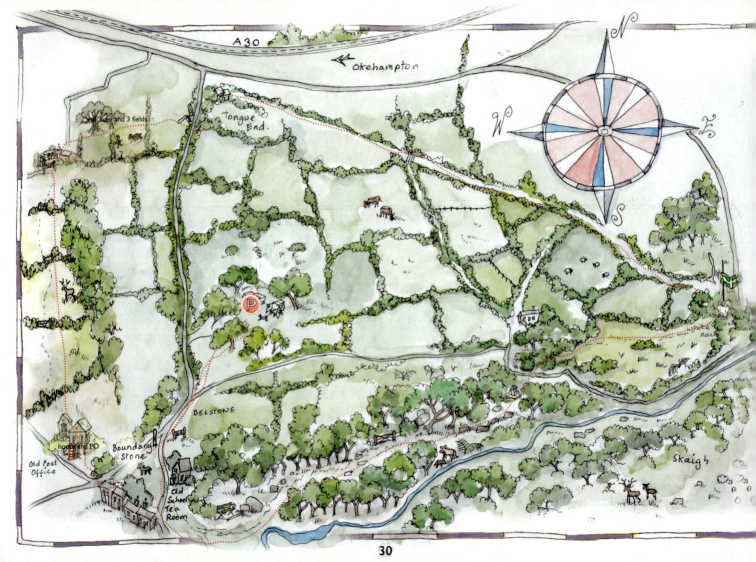

Belstone Cleave

DISTANCE *Approximately 6km (3.7miles)* **TIME** *Approximately 1.5hrs.*
DIFFICULTY *A fairly easy walk with varied terrain and muddy in places.*
///**WHAT3WORDS** *berated.displays.slept or SX621938*
WINNIE SAYS *this is a* 🐾🐾

A circular one from Belstone car park, taking in Belstone Cleave, Skaigh, Tongue End and Priestacott, and is ideal if you need a sheltered walk from the sun or the rain…the rain being more likely! It can however, be quite muddy in places after heavy rain. It is a lovely varied walk along tracks, fields and meadows.

Turn left out of the car park on Brenamoor Common and follow the road around the right hand bend passing the **Belstone Stocks** and **Belstone Pound** on your left.

Belstone Stocks

On reaching the grass triangle and the Standing Stone, take the left fork, passing by the Old School Tea Rooms. You will come on to the common sloping down hill to your left. Stay close to the hedge here and start walking down hill where you will see a seat on your left and a small path. Take this path which is level and follows the wall behind the houses at the top of **Belstone Cleave**. There are amazing views across the valley on your right hand side towards **Cosdon Beacon**.

Walks with Winnie

The seat at the start of the Cleave path and the Belstone Manor Pound sign

Look out for violets along the woodland path in spring

The path takes you through a tunnel of trees which has a feel of the 'Jungle' but be aware it can get very muddy at times and there may be cows with calves: so stay alert. Continue on this path which becomes a bit tricky towards the end where you meet another track joining from the right. Turn left and up towards the road. You will see a lovely fountain with drinking water, just at the right time for the dog!

Once on the corner of the road turn right down the hill passing the bench on your left, the fence and wall on your right. Next to a big tree and a small stream on your left, there is a gravel path that will take you up the hill, (it looks like you are walking up a small stream to start with) away from the road. Follow this now until it becomes level and you can see the top of the trees in the Skaigh Valley below. At the end of the path you will reach a small gate, during the winter without the leaves on the trees you will see **White Rock** where the Minister would preach to the folk of Sticklepath. Turn left up the hill, meeting a path joining from the right, continue left along this narrow path and through the 5 bar gate.

The track now widens, stay on this, passing a stable on your right and a large house on your left. At the next gate and cattle grid continue straight on to Tongue End and the main road. On reaching the road, turn left walking about 50m, take the foot path on the

The Lion's Mouth Drinking Fountain

Belstone Cleave

Looking towards Belstone Tor and cream tea at the Old School Tea Rooms

right, over the stile and in to the open field. At this point the walk feels very different out in the open. Walk through the middle of the next 3 fields heading for the large Oak Tree. The next gate will be in front of you. This path will now bring you into Priestacott. Turn left on the road and take the second foot path sign on your left through the court yard of the house. The path is to the right of the house and brings you into a field. Stay to the right and follow the signs, through fields and meadows, through gates and stiles. This area can again be wet and muddy after rain. You will be amazed where this path comes out! Turn left on the road and you are now back in Belstone and if you have timed it right, the 'Old School Tea Rooms' may be open or The Tors Inn.

Did you know...

Around 1875 William Symington of Rockside Estate, bought 88 acres of mixed woodland at Skaigh Wood, laying out riverside paths and building the Lion's Head Drinking Fountain. which is still running today. However, the water may not be suitable for drinking.

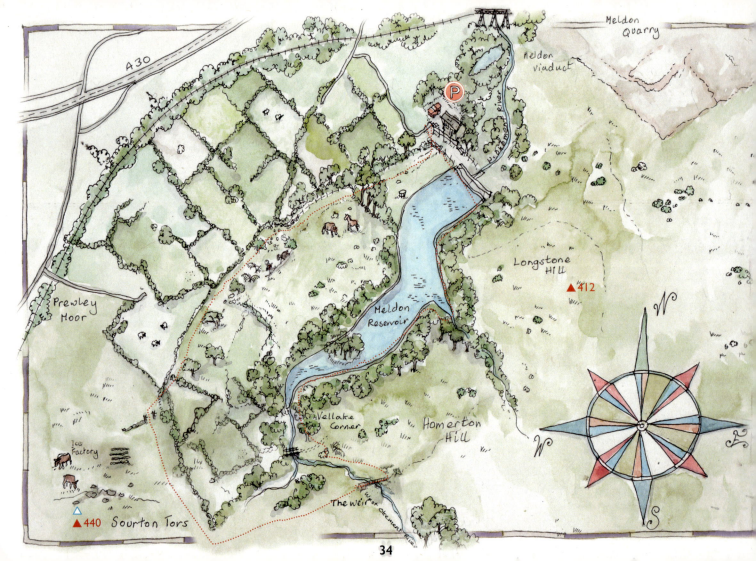

Meldon Reservoir

> **DISTANCE** *Approximately 6km (3.7miles)* **TIME** *Approximately 1.5hrs.*
> **DIFFICULTY** *This is a walk of varied terrain and width of path which can be stoney and slippy in places. Part of the track from Meldon car park can be muddy at times.*
> ///**WHAT3WORDS** *proofread.single.infringe or SX562917*
> **WINNIE SAYS** *this is a* 🐾🐾

We have for you a lovely circular walk from Meldon Car Park, taking in the open moors near Sourton Tors, **Vellake Corner,** the Nature Reserve and **Meldon Reservoir**. Although you or your dogs are not permitted to swim in the reservoir, there are places along the Okement River that feeds it where you can swim. There is no shelter on this walk and it is very open in places.

A first glimpse of the reservoir

From Meldon Car Park take the steps up to the road and immediately on to the foot path opposite heading up hill. Take a moment to look back at the amazing views of the reservoir and Tors beyond.

The second footpath sign will be at the tree line where the path runs parallel to the stone wall on your right. Stay with this path as it contours along the side of South Down bringing you out into the open.

Walks with Winnie

Looking across to the river and Homerton hill

your left where it now starts to head down the hill and forks in front of you. Take the left fork slightly down hill where looking ahead you will see the track opposite you as it contours around. Continue to walk along the path, contouring around the edge of the hill to the stream.

Cross the stream following the track at the same level around the side of the hill. You can clearly see the track continuing in front of you slightly up and crossing a second stream. This path is now very narrow, taking you down to the left around the edge of the valley and down where you will start to see the open flat plains of the nature reserve and the West Okement River heading towards the reservoir. The power

West Okement River

Head towards the stone wall in front of you and bear left towards the gate. You will see Sourton Tors and the **Ice Factory** in the distance. The pathway here is easy to follow but can be muddy when it's wet. Follow the path to the gate and onto the open moors.

As you come out onto the moors keeping the stone wall on your left, head toward a gate post at the end of the wall. Turn left at this point keeping the wall on

house at the weir will come into sight, head towards this and cross the river. A great spot for swimming in the summer for you and your dog!

Having crossed the river, head straight across to the track (you will see a wide track joining from the right and up hill, ignore this for now) turning left head toward the reservoir and the trees. The path can be clearly seen and will now take you up a short incline and right along the side of the reservoir all the way back to the car park. As you walk along this path, take a look across to the island, where if the water levels are low you almost feel you could walk out there. There are nesting birds here if you look closely.

You will finally arrive at the dam with views down toward Meldon Viaduct where during an episode of 'Mission with Bear Grylls" the explorer took comedian David Walliams on an expedition on Dartmoor. He had to climb Meldon Viaduct as well as abseil down Meldon Quarry. An episode well worth watching!

The island in the middle of the reservoir is a sanctuary for birds such as kingfishers.

Did you know...

There were early signs of humans living on Dartmoor in the Mesolithic period 10,000BC-4000BC. They would have exploited the forests and environment for food, although they left little physical trace, except for stone tools they would have used.

Nordic walkers on Belstone Tor

- Whiddon Deer Park
- Cosdon Beacon
- Halstock Bluebell Woods
- Fatherford
- High Willhays
- Cornridge WWII Plane Crash Site

Whiddon Deer Park

> **DISTANCE** Approximately 4.5km (2.8miles) **TIME** Approximately 1hr 15mins. allowing time to stop and admire the view.
> **DIFFICULTY** Mostly flat apart from one steep hill.
> **///WHAT3WORDS** replayed.moped.swinging or SX713893
> **WINNIE SAYS** this is a 🐾🐾🐾

A circular walk starting at Dogmarsh Bridge near the Mill End Hotel, Chagford, following the River Teign. Great places for you and the dog to swim!

Park along side the road after **Dogmarsh Bridge** and the Mill End Hotel on your left. It can get very busy here in the summer months and at weekends.

With the River Teign on your right hand side, take the gate into the open field (this is where the annual **Chagford Show** takes place in August, certainly worth seeing) following the path passing a bridge on your right hand side, continue to the field gate in front of you. As you pass through this gate you will be able to see **Castle Drogo** up on the hill top on your left hand side.

Stay on this path until you reach the next gate, taking the suspension bridge on your right to cross the river. This is **Drew's Weir** a great spot if you like to wild swimming, you can almost swim lengths!

Mill End Hotel

41

Walks with Winnie

Peter Randall-Page sculpture named 'Passage'

level out and you come to a tree lined avenue which takes you through an opening in the stone wall with 'Passage', a **Peter Randall-Page** sculpture at each side of this entrance.

Continue on the path to the top looking to your left where you will see Castle Drogo. Follow the path to the right through the woods and out into the open. The views from here are worth the climb and you may be lucky enough to see the white deer. Also, there is a shepherd's hut which you will pass. With the hut on

The shepherd's hut with bluebells and Chagford in the distance

Take the path up the stone steps and over the wall. On the other side of the wall you have 2 choices. If you don't mind a steep climb take the narrow path directly in front of you and up the slope. Alternatively, turn left, and after a few feet take the path up the slope on your right; a more gentle climb.

Staying on this narrow path you will start to climb uphill and into the woods. This is where it starts to get steep. This path can be muddy during wet weather but the climb will be worth it for sure. Just when you think you have had enough, the path starts to

Whiddon Deer Park

Crabapple trees in full bloom

your left continue on the path where it is all down hill from here! Through the woods the path winds its way down the hill. As you reach the path at the bottom turn right until you come to the stone bridge on your left hand side. Cross the bridge through the gate following the path winding to the left. On the right after Whiddon House head through the gate. This is a narrow path between the woods and the fields known locally as Blood Lane. At the end of the path take the steps to the right down towards the river. Turn left out of the gate until you reach the bridge. Crossing this, turn left again into the open fields. You will now see Dogmarsh Bridge in front of you and the start of the walk.

Dogmarsh Bridge crossing over the River Teign where you often see Kayakers

Did you know...

The lowest point on Dartmoor is Dog Hole Bridge in the Teign Valley; 30m or 98 feet above sea level.

43

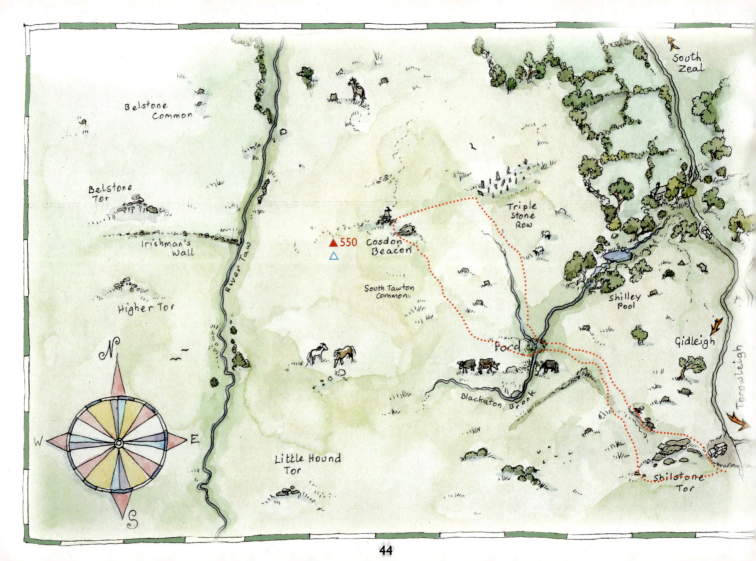

Cosdon Beacon

> **DISTANCE** *Approximately 6km (3.7miles)* **TIME** *Approximately 2+hrs.*
> **DIFFICULTY** *Starting with a flattish walk, then uphill all the way to the Beacon. It's downhill all the way back.*
> ///**WHAT3WORDS** *agreement.obvious.brings or SX659902*
> **WINNIE SAYS** *this is a* 🐾🐾🐾

This is an open walk with no shelter from the sun or rain! Not recommended as a dog walk on a hot day although you do cross Blackaton Brook a couple of times. It is a steady up hill to **Cosdon Beacon** (550m) from Shilstone Tor (314m), becoming steeper as you get closer to it. On the way back you will take in the **Cosdon Hill Triple Stone Row**. But then of course…it is down hill all the way back!

View towards Cosdon Beacon

It is a walk that is definitely worth the climb as the views from the top are far reaching towards Haytor, Exmoor and beyond.

Park at the base of Shilstone Tor and walk up towards the Tor. Behind the Tor and with the Tor to your back you will see Cosdon Beacon in the far distance and a track taking you in to the moors through Throwleigh Common. Stay on this track for about 10 minutes where you will see a row of bushes in front of you. Take the

Walks with Winnie

Triple Stone Row

track to your left before you reach them where it will run towards the opposite end of the line of bushes which should always be on your right.

Once you reach the row of bushes head straight across and down the hill towards Blackaton Brook and the ford. A good spot for the dog to paddle or even swim if we have had rain!

Passing over the stream you will see a track in front of you which contours around the side of Kennon Hill to the right. Follow this track until you meet another stream, crossing over this and staying on the track up towards a dry leat. A nice flat spot to stop before the final ascent to the top! Even the views from here are pretty extraordinary with Castle Drogo easy to spot in the distance.

Continue up hill now, a steady climb staying on the track all the way to the top. It is one of those climbs where it feels like you are always "Nearly there"!

Cosdon Beacon and the **Trig point** will be a welcome sight here at Cosdon Hill on South Tawton Common. The views are far reaching. It is worth the climb. You will also see many **Cairns.** This is where those Nordic Walking poles come into their own! Stay a while and take in the 360 degree view. It always makes us want to carry on walking further into the moors and reach the next Tor,…but we will save that for another day.

Blackaton Brook

View of Cosdon Beacon

46

Bog Asphodel in the early summer brighten up the peat bogs

Cosdon Beacon

Head back down starting with the Beacon behind you. Face towards the direction you have come. You will be able to make out a grass covered stone circle in front of you. To the left of this you will see a grass track heading down hill, take this and as you walk over the ridge you will clearly see the Triple Stone Row down and slightly to your left. Standing at the top end of the row looking straight ahead, you can see a wide track towards your right, and in the distance in line with the stone row you can see Castle Drogo. Staying on this for about 300m, a further track on your right will take you back towards the Blackaton Brook in the valley. Crossing over the stream you will be faced with several tracks, take the one on the right. At the start of this track you will find a small piece of triangular shaped granite; it points in the direction you need to go… We have put this here as a reminder for us and call it the "Cheese", you will see why! Once over the brow of the hill you will once again see the line of bushes. The path heads towards the left hand corner of this. With the bushes on your right this time, heading continually down hill, stay on the track back to Shilstone Tor. Looking up and to your right you will see Kestor in the distance and on a clear day Haytor too.

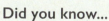

The 'cheese' to direct you

Did you know...

The English Cocker is one of the oldest of land spaniels and can be traced back to 14th century Spain. Before the 1600's spaniels were categorised together; the larger ones being used to spring game and the smaller ones to flush out woodcock. Hence the names Springer and Cocker.

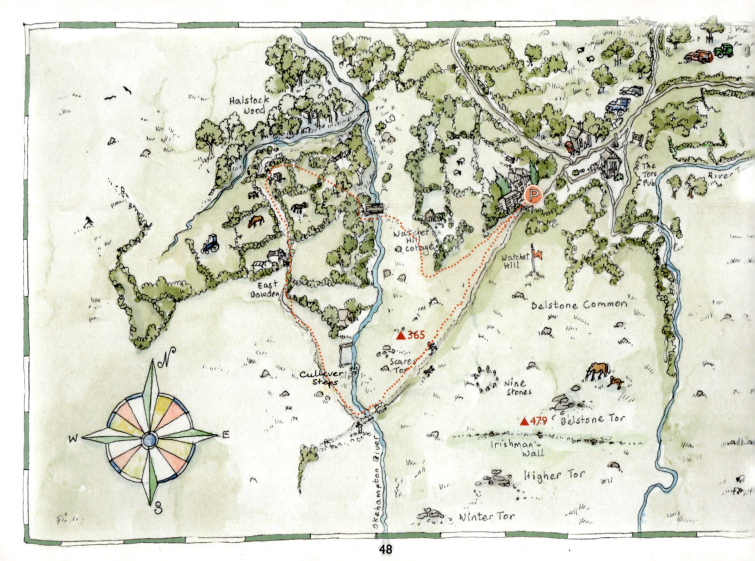

Halstock Bluebell Woods

> **DISTANCE** *Approximately 6km (3.7miles).* **TIME** *Approximately 1.5hrs.*
> **DIFFICULTY** *An undulating walk with a climb from the East Okement River up on to the open moors and amazing bluebell woods.*
> ///**WHAT3WORDS** *backtrack.weeks.scarves or SX616933.*
> **WINNIE SAYS** *this is a* 🐾🐾🐾

An undulating walk with hills, moors, and an amazing bluebell woods!

This is a circular walk starting at Belstone Waterworks, taking in Halstock (the bluebell) woods, Lower Halstock Farm and **Cullever Steps** - a great place for a wild swim. Partly sheltered with lots of places for you and the dog to swim.

By the Waterworks, take the gate out onto the moors. Up and to your left is Watchet Hill with the flag pole and Belstone Common beyond. It is safe to do this walk even if the red flag is flying. The red flag will be flying if there is firing on the moors. (You can check this on the **Dartmoor Firing times site**). Follow the gravel track alongside the wall. When you arrive at the corner take the grass track to your right to the opposite corner at the end of the wall, and head straight down the hill (from the corner of this wall the track on your left will take you directly to the Nine Stones).

The red flag will be flying when there is firing practice on the moors

Walks with Winnie

As you come over the brow of the hill in front of you, you will see the East Okement River below and a track crossing your path right to left. Walk over this track heading down towards the river where you will pick up a narrow gravel track heading down to your right. Keep on this track with the river on your left. The track slowly angles closer to the river. You will arrive at the bridge and a flat area which is very popular for camping. Cross the small bridge by the ford and into the Bluebells of Halstock Wood, an amazing site, so try and take this walk in late spring. It is well worth a visit.

After crossing the bridge, turn right and

Halstock wood

Bluebells

Looking back at the bridge

follow the track which gradually starts to go up hill. This is part of the **Tarka Trail**. It can be a bit rough in places. Coming to a post with markers on at a junction, take the track up hill to your left (the path right is the continuation of the Tarka Trail) continuing through the woods and eventually a gate into the open. The path continues to follow the wall which will now be on your left hand side, bringing you into a small section of woods. Head through the gate, where you will see a cottage on your left. The path then tracks through a small field and into the yard of Halstock Farm. Take the path to your left, up the hill through a couple of

Halstock Bluebell Woods

Halstock Farm

River once again, the ford and Cullever steps; a natural pool, great for a wild swim!

Cross the river now staying on the track and heading left. Continue on this track all the way back to the water works at Belstone, passing Scarey Tor on your left. You can detour up to the Tor with views down into the valley and across to the path you have just walked down.

gates, and onto the open moors at East Bowden. Turn left at the corner of the wall. Stay on this track heading for a small stone wall with trees (don't take the path that forks left).

Walking along you will now see the open moor and Belstone Tor to your left, with Winter and Higher Tor in front of you. The track will now take you downhill towards the East Okement

Looking across the valley from Nine Stones

Did you know....

Bluebells are protected under the Wildlife and Countryside Act 1981. If you dig up wild bluebells you can be heavily fined.

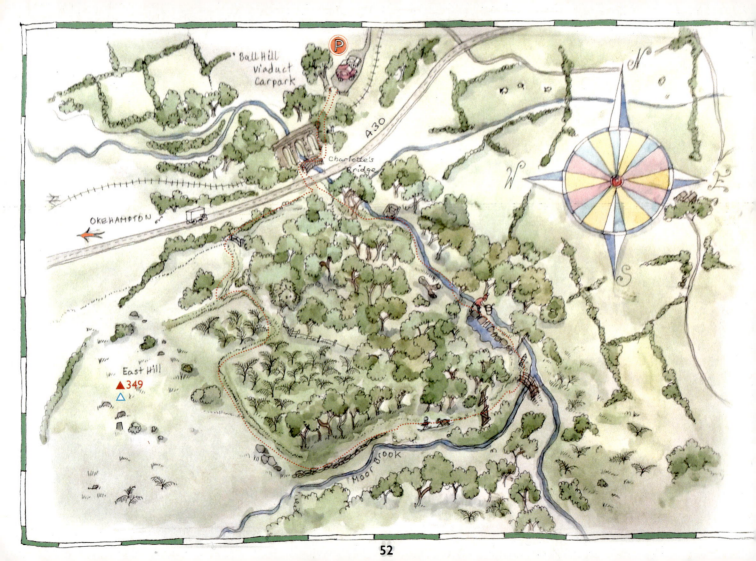

Fernworthy reservoir

Fatherford

> **DISTANCE** Approximately 4km (2.5miles) **TIME** Approximately 1hr.
> **DIFFICULTY** The terrain can be slippy. There are stepping stones to negotiate and a steep narrow path up through the woods. The stepping stones are impassable when the river is high.
> ///**what3words** tiling.workroom.renting or SX603949
> **WINNIE SAYS** this is a

A circular walk from Fatherford Bridge, along the East Okement River and up towards East Hill. The Ladies from Dartmoor Nordic Walking have named this walk 'The Goat Track'! From Fatherford along the East Okement River is part of the Tarka Trail.

This walk starts at the car park by Fatherford Bridge. A flat start along the river, it has narrow paths and a climb up towards East Hill. It can be hazardous after heavy rain as part of the path becomes stepping stones and may be impassable. However, during the summer, it is a great walk for the dogs as there are plenty of places to swim!

From the car park, pass though the gate towards the river taking **'Charlotte's Bridge'**, then left through the gate towards the East Okement Valley. Pass under the bridges taking either the left path walking directly next to the river or the right hand path through the woods (ignore the sign pointing up towards a steep hill beside

Fatherford Bridge

Walks with Winnie

A good resting log

Stepping stones and pool to the right. A good place to spot little tadpoles

tadpoles

the bridge, we will be coming back this way). This is a mostly flat walk at this point following the river, which will always be on your left. You will come across a very large fallen tree log, a great place to sit and rest whilst you watch the dogs swimming! This path is now part of the new **Dartmoor Way** and also the **Tarka Trail.**

From here you now approach the stepping stones, be careful as they can sometimes be slippy. Keep an eye out for the tadpoles along the right hand side as you cross. Continue along until you reach a bridge on your left, at this point take the right hand path up the hill and over the stile. The path now becomes more uneven and steeper; not a problem if you have your Nordic Poles with you! The woods here are full of amazing colours all year round. The path becomes narrow, with the river and the stone wall on your left. Follow the wall until

Denise is pointing to the Dartmoor Way symbol. A new path that opened October 2020

it finishes. Head up the hill to the right until you reach the corner of the wall on your left bringing you out on to the open moorland.

The path from here is out in the open. With your back to the corner of the wall, head down the wide track between the single trees. The path then bends to the right and becomes nice and wide. Continue towards a gate in the wire fence and field in front of you. Turn left here; don't go through the gate. The path then heads down the hill, through the gorse, and between a few holly trees, reaching a second path (there will be another gate on you right; don't go through this one either). Turn left and after approximately 20 feet, turn right down the hill between the large trees. This bit is steep. At the bottom of this hill go through the gate on your right. Another steep descent joining the path where you started. Turn left under the bridges and back to the car park.

See the glorious colours of the woodland in Autumn whilst you're crossing Charlotte's Bridge

Did you know...

Along side the stepping stones during March or April time, you might see tadpoles and sometimes newts in the these ponds.

High Willhays

DISTANCE *Approximately 6k (3.8 miles)* **TIME** *Approximately 2 hours.*
DIFFICULTY *A steady up hill, more noticeable just before reaching Yes Tor. Terrain mostly gravel with clear paths the majority of the way.*
///**WHAT3WORDS** *patch.clerk.active or SX591912*
WINNIE SAYS *this is a* 🐾🐾🐾

From Okehampton Army camp and Moor Gate, turn right on to the Ranges and drive as far as you can along the tarmac road. You will clearly see where you can park, it is only a small area. If you park facing the way you have come, West Mill Tor is on your left hand side.

This is a great walk with amazing views throughout. It is very open so make sure you take the correct clothing for the conditions.

View across to Cosdon Beacon

It is a there-and-back walk, but you can take a detour up to Yes Tor. The path will take you over a small stream, suitable for cooling off the dog!

With West Mill Tor on your right hand side, follow the gravel path in front of you, not to the left, this path would take you to Rowtor. As you make your way along this path, on your left you will see the firing range and what looks like a hut. This is the Locomotive shed for the Wickham

Walks with Winnie

A bit of uphill now to a point where the ground starts to flatten out, where you will then see a track to the left as you get closer to Yes Tor. If you stay on the track which bends around to the right, you will reach Yes Tor which you can see clearly in front of you now. We are heading left from this track where you will see a range of granite Tors in front of you on the horizon, the furthest being High Willhays (621m) the highest Tor on Dartmoor. The views from here are amazing. Standing with Yes Tor to your left you can see Steeperton Tor in front of you, to the left of that Oke Tor, Belstone Tor and the ridge. Turning to face the opposite way, on your far left Great Links Tor and Corn ridge in front of this. Along and below here is a WWII plane crash site with a further WWII plane crash site at Corn Ridge *(See pages 60-63)*.

Rowtor looking towards Rowtor target railway *(right)*

Trolleys that were used for military target practice. This is the **Rowtor target railway** opened in 1959 and still there today. The tracks are still easily visible.

Continue along the track, and then take the right fork where there's a slight incline flattening out when you can see Yes Tor (619 m). Stay on the track crossing a small stream, a great place for the dog to have a drink and to cool your feet on a warm day.

58

High Willhays

A trig point looking from Yes Tor to High Willhays where sometimes you can see the buzzards circling

Following the ridge along you will see Sourton Tor and the site of the Sourton Ice Factory…yes Ice factory!

   Stay and enjoy the view for as far as you can see. Have a coffee, and when you are ready take a deep breath, head back down the way you have come enjoying the views on your descent.

A painting by David Lewin of Yes Tor

Did you know…

It was thought originally that Yes Tor was the highest Tor on Dartmoor, but thanks to modern surveying technology it lost its crown by 2m to High Willhays

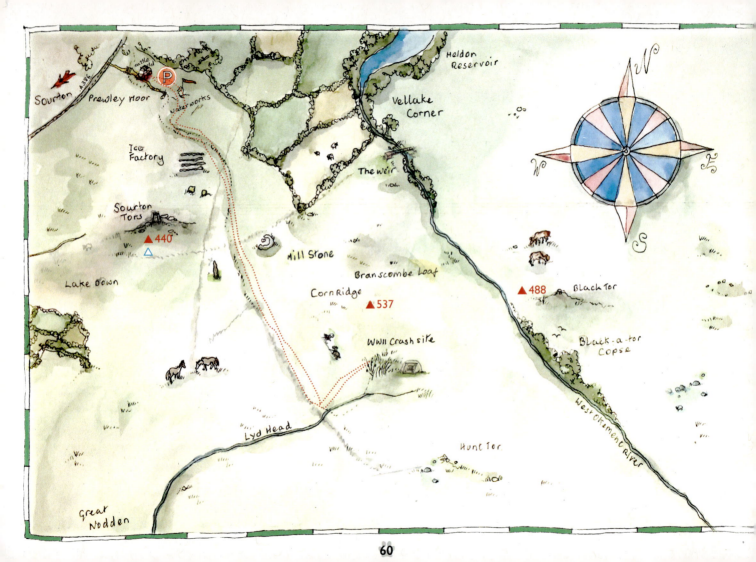

Cornridge WWII Plane Crash Site

DISTANCE *Approximately 7.5k (4.7 miles)* **TIME** *Allow 2.5hrs minimum.*
DIFFICULTY *Up hill from the start, down hill all the way back! Terrain is mostly soft and grassy, but can be wet and boggy near the crash site.*
///**WHAT3WORDS** *hissing.lecturers.notched or SX545910*
WINNIE SAYS *this is a* 🐾🐾🐾

This is a there-and-back walk with lots to see on the way to the WWII crash site. It is an open moor walk so be aware of the weather, take appropriate clothing and equipment.

Park at Prewley Moor below Sourton Tors. There are several parking areas here.

Head out up the hill towards the left and flatter area of Sourton Tors. There are several paths you can take which will lead you up to the **Ice Factory.** Yes, ice works on Dartmoor! You can see the remains of the undulating cut outs which will be on your right below the Tor. Once you reach the flatter terrain, you will pass through the remains of 2 stone pillars. Head up the hill between them.

Staying to the left of the tor, follow the wide pathway taking you up hill again where the ground then begins to flatten out. Head straight across the tracks passing the

The Ice Factory remains

Walks with Winnie

The Half Mill Stone

Cotton grass, a common sight on Dartmoor

Staying on the gravel track, head towards Great Links Tor clearly visible in the distance…another walk for another day!

You are now looking to head to a point where you reach a stream flowing under the path. It can be deep in places, a good spot to cool off the dogs and your feet on a hot day. Don't cross over the stream.

Nordic walkers on Sourton Tors and Great Nodden in the background *(below)*

boundary stone on your right and The Half Mill Stone on your left. As you look back and to your left you can see Meldon Reservoir, 'Black Tor', 'High Willhays' (the highest Tor on Dartmoor) and 'Yes Tor' to its left.

Keep going straight, slowly walking up hill again and to the right around the base of Corn Ridge. The path here is quite wide but keep a look out for a narrower path on your left, taking you up and over a small brow bringing you out on a gravel track which is clearly visible.

You can now see Great Nodden in front of you with very steep sides and a lovely path leading to its summit…this is a walk for another day!

Cornridge WWII Plane Crash Site

At this point you will be walking off the track to your left, keeping the stream on your right. The path here is not clear so you will need to take care as it can be boggy and uneven. The crash site is hard to find, but if you do find it....great job!

Walking at about a 45 degree angle from the stream, still keeping it on your right, follow the tracks which lead you toward a boggy area. If you skirt around this to the left but look across it to the right, you will see a dark area in the ground with a slight bank around the far edge. Keep a note of the way you have come, as you will be heading back the same way. This is the crash site. Pick your way carefully towards it. You will know you have found the site as there is a large area of parched ground and a small metal memorial plaque as shown in the photo. It has the names of the Crew of the stricken flight boeing B-17G Flying Fortress. They were the 8th Air Force USAAF. Five of whom sadly lost their lives, and three who survived on that fateful Christmas Day 1943, heading back home. An interesting fact: this plaque is actually made from part of the plane.

You have reached your destination, so about turn and head back to the car the way you came once more enjoying the views. It always looks like a new walk on the way back.

The B-17G Flying Fortress; a four engined heavy bomber

The metal memorial plaque at the crash site.
(This is a sacred site and war grave with historic significance. No artefacts of this nature should be removed or tampered with)

Did you know...

Branscombe's Loaf is supposedly a petrified meal of bread (loaf) and cheese offered by the devil in disguise as a stranger, to Walter Branscombe, bishop of Exeter in the 13th century, whilst he was riding home one night with his chaplin.

View from Yes Tor to West Mill Tor

Glossary

Glossary

BELSTONE CLEAVE Is a wooded steep sided valley between Belstone and Sticklepath, which has the River Taw running through it.

BELSTONE POUND Belstone Manor Pound was used to contain stray or illegally pastured livestock. The fines paid for their release would go to the Lord of the Manor.

BELSTONE STOCKS Used it is said for offences against the Church or infringing common laws. Last used in 1800's? Now a grade II listed feature.

BLACKATON BROOK Source from Raybarrow pool, through Shilley Pool meandering near Gidleigh Mill and the "War Cleave"

COSDON BEACON 550m (1800ft) above sea level. Also know as Cosdon Hill and Cawsand Beacon. There is a Cairn and Trig point here too.

CASTLE DROGO The last Castle to be built in England for Julian Drewe between 1911 and 1930. It is now a National Trust property.

CAIRN A pile of stones possibly used in modern times for navigation, but date back to the Bronze Age, which could have been used as memorials or boundary markers. Artefacts have been found on some Cairns.

CULLEVER STEPS A natural pool on the East Okehampton River near Scarey Tor, Belstone

CHAGFORD SHOW The Chagford Agricultural and Horticultural show is a traditional one day country show. It is held each year on the third Thursday in August. It was established in the 1900's.

CHARLOTTE'S BRIDGE In memory of 12 year old Charlotte Saunders, who tragically lost her life whilst crossing the swollen river when her pony bucked. A safe way to cross the river for walkers and horse riders.

CLAPPER BRIDGE An ancient bridge found on Dartmoor, made of large slabs of granite.

COSDON HILL TRIPLE STONE ROW Around 146-176 m in length. Headed by a Cairn, two Cist's were found in it. There are roughly five Triple Stone Rows on Dartmoor. There is no real agreement as to why they were built.

Glossary

Fernworthy Reservoir on a calm day

CRANBROOK CASTLE HILL FORT An Iron Age Hill Fort overlooking the Teign Valley.

DARTMOOR FIRING TIMES: GOV.UK A list of training areas and firing times on Dartmoor.

DARTMOOR NATIONAL PARK Has had National Park Heritage since 1951. It is 954 Km^2 (368 miles^2). It is managed by the Dartmoor National Park Authority (DNPA) which was created in 1995.

DARTMOOR WAY A 108 mile (173km) circular walking route around Dartmoor, opened October 2020, linking local villages, towns and hamlets. There is an additional 22.5 mile high moor route. There is also a 95 mile cycle route.

DREWS WEIR A natural pool below Castle Drogo, suitable for fishing, swimming. The weir is also a salmon leap.

DOGMARSH BRIDGE Also known as Sandy Bridge. A granite built bridge over the River Teign near Chagford, Sandy Park.

FERNWORTHY FOREST Managed by Forestry England. Covers 576 Hectares, and was first planted by the Duchy of Cornwall in 1921.

FERNWORTHY RESERVOIR Near Chagford. Built between 1936-1942. Managed by South West Lakes Trust, it feeds Torquay, Totnes and Brixham. There are lots of ancient settlements around here.

FERNWORTHY CIRCLE One of the "Sacred Crescent" of stone circles on Dartmoor. Also knows as Froggymead, a Bronze Age Circle with 27 Granite slabs.

HUNTER'S TOR Above the River Teign and below Castle Drogo. Not a very high Tor, but has great views towards Sharp Tor and on the Hunters Path.

HUNTERS PATH A path near Castle Drogo high above the River Teign. Taking in the woods and farmland.

ICE FACTORY SOURTON Also know as "Sourton Ponds" Built in 1875 to collect water and store the ice for the winter, using Bridestow Railway Station, taking it to Plymouth for fishermen to preserve their catch.

IRISHMAN'S WALL An enclosure built by Irish labourers in the early 1800's. Reaching from Cullever Steps, over Belstone Ridge and down the other side. It is said that the locals destroyed it to stop their commoners rights being taken away as Dartmoor was slowly becoming enclosed.

KIST/KISTVAEN/CIST A four sided Burial tomb, late Neolithic or Early Bronze age.

LEAT A man made water way used to transport water. off the moor.

LONGSTON Near Kestor, A megalith (prehistoric monument) for example a standing stone. A terminal stone for the Bronze Age stone row and more recently used as a boundary stone.

METHERALL HUT CIRCLES At Fernworthy Reservoir. A set of 7 prehistoric hut circles, larger than those usually found on Dartmoor. There are a few that can only be seen in the summer or when the water level is low.

MELDON RESERVOIR 900ft above sea level. Managed by South West Lakes Trust. Built in September 1974.

MELDON VIADUCT Carried the London and South Western Railway across the West Okement River. It was opened in 1874.

NATIONAL TRUST Founded 12th January 1895 and is now Europes largest conservation charity caring for historic properties.

NINE STONES BELSTONE Also knows as Nine Maidens or the Seventeen Brothers. Bronze Age stone circle. A burial chamber where the Cairn had been robbed and a cist destroyed.

PETER RANDALL-PAGE A world renowned artist. There are 2 Sculptures in Chagford. "Granite song" (1991)on the Two Moors way near Millend Hotel, and "Passage" (1992) at Whiddon Deer Park.

POTTERS WALK A wheelchair/ pushchair friendly walk, flat and easy. 0.75mile circular walk. Built 1993 and named after Sydney Potter who lived and worked at Fernworthy for over 50 years.

ROCK BASIN There are quite a few on Dartmoor, Kestor in particular. Have they been made by nature and localised weathering or, by the Druids to collect "pure water" or to catch blood from sacrifices?

Glossary

Winnie at Nine Maidens, also known as Nine Stones, Belstone

ROWTOR TARGET RAILWAY Built in 1959 a 30" gauge railway, 450m long. An engine pulled a target along the track for firing practice.

SCORHILL STONE CIRCLE Also know as Gidleigh Circle and Steep Hill Circle, one of 14 on Dartmoor. Has been called the "Stonehenge of Dartmoor". A possible meeting place, from the Bronze Age.

SHOVEL DOWN Near Kestor. A ceremonial site with many stone rows, Cairn circles, and standing stones.

TARKA TRAIL 180 miles of track ways, the longest off road cycle path in the UK. Passes through Sticklepath, Belstone and Okehampton. Following the route of Tarka the Otter.

THREE BOYS STANDING STONE Only 1 left standing now. Dating back to the Bronze Age an end stone marking the Southern end of the stone row

TOLMEN STONE A large boulder with a naturally occurring hole formed by river erosion, big enough for an adult to pass through. Said to "cure rheumatic disorders" or "can get you pregnant" if you can climb through it!

TRIG POINT OR Triangulation points, were built by Ordnance Survey in 1936 to map the country. There were 6500 built. Usually on high points, you will find them shown on a map as a triangle. You can see one at Yes Tor.

TWO CASTLES TRAIL A 24mile (38km) trail linking two Norman Castles in Okehampton and Launceston. Follows part of the West Devon Way.

VELLAKE CORNER At the top end of Meldon Reservoir, near the Packhorse Bridge and the Weir on the West Okement River. Also a nature reserve.

WEST DEVON WAY A 35mile route along the Western Edge of Dartmoor from Okehampton to Hooe Lake, Plymouth.

WHIDDON/WHYDDON DEER PARK Near Chagford. Created in 1570 by Sir John Whyddon who owned Whyddon House. A sautés symbol with fallow deer and high boundary walls.

WHITE ROCK Sticklepath, with a flag pole and the Devon flag. In the 1700's a Methodist Preacher John Wesley, would. preach to the village from this spot.

Acknowedgements

To all of the dogs who have been part of my life and helped me realise I love walking on Dartmoor with a four legged friend by my side. I would not be me without a dog. Winnie has been the inspiration for the walks as she is always with me. However, Diesel My Chocolate Labrador helped me discover many walks on Dartmoor over the years as did Holly who lived with us on the moors.

In putting together this book, many sources of information were used from the original walks publicised in the "Walks with Winnie' section of the Oke Links magazine. Thank you to Jane Honey, Editor of the Oke Links magazine for getting me to finally put pen to paper since 2016.

To the readers of the Oke Links, many of who have told me, the "Walks with Winnie" is the first section they go to, to those who have told me they have followed the walks, and to those walkers who we have met who have recognised Winnie!

To my Nordic Walking groups who have tried and tested many of walks with me and made me realise how much I enjoy exploring the moors with people and helping them become familiar with Dartmoor.

Also to Sara Nunan, who has made my ideas a reality. I love everything about the book and have never felt so excited about a new idea. Thank you Sara.

Dartmoor hill ponies
(opposite)